The Servant Leader's Playbook:
A Guide to Effective Leadership for All

Dr. Jose A. Mendez

The Servant's Leader Playbook:

A Guide to Effective Leadership for All

ISBN: 9798854090742

The Servant's Leader Playbook:

A Guide to Effective Leadership for All

DEDICATION

To those in the pursuit of knowledge, never stop learning, for it is through learning that we build the solid foundation of our lives.

The Servant's Leader Playbook:

A Guide to Effective Leadership for All

ACKNOWLEDGMENTS

Thank you to the ones who have supported me even when my crazy ideas made only sense to me and no one else. You know who you are, and all mean the world to me.

The Servant's Leader Playbook:

A Guide to Effective Leadership for All

Contents

Chapter 1
Understanding Servant Leadership

Defining Servant Leadership

Servant leadership is a philosophy and approach to leadership that focuses on serving the needs of others first and foremost. It is a concept that has gained significant traction in the business world in recent years as more and more organizations realize the value of putting their employees and customers at the center of their operations. At its core, servant leadership is about empowering and supporting others to reach their full potential. It is not about wielding power or authority but rather about using one's position to facilitate growth and development in others. In essence, a servant leader prioritizes the well-being and success of their team members and is willing to go above and beyond to ensure their needs are met.

One of the fundamental principles of servant leadership is empathy. A

The Servant's Leader Playbook:

A Guide to Effective Leadership for All

servant leader is someone who can understand and share the feelings of others and is genuinely interested in their concerns and aspirations. Servant leaders create trust and open communication by practicing active listening and showing natural care and concern for their team members. Another important aspect of servant leadership is humility. Servant leaders recognize that they are not the sole source of knowledge or expertise and are willing to learn from others and admit when they are wrong. This humility allows them to foster a collaborative and inclusive work environment where everyone's ideas and contributions are valued.

Servant leadership also emphasizes the importance of ethical conduct and social responsibility. A servant leader acts with integrity, always making decisions that are in the best interests of their team and the organization as a whole. They also recognize their responsibility to the broader community and actively seek opportunities to make a positive impact.

Servant leadership is a powerful and transformative approach to leadership that puts the needs of others first. It is about creating a supportive and empowering environment where individuals can thrive and reach their full potential. By practicing empathy, humility, and ethical conduct, servant leaders inspire excellence in their teams and drive organizational success.

Historical Background of Servant Leadership

Servant leadership, as a concept, has its roots in ancient civilizations and has resonated throughout history in various forms. Understanding the historical background of servant leadership provides CEOs, leaders, and managers with invaluable insights into its evolution and relevance in today's business landscape. One of the earliest examples of servant leadership can be traced back to the teachings of the ancient Chinese philosopher Lao Tzu. Lao Tzu's philosophy emphasized leading by serving and empowering others. His teachings on humility, compassion, and selflessness laid the foundation for a leadership style that prioritized the needs of others above one's own.

In the Western world, the concept of servant leadership gained prominence during the Renaissance period. Renaissance thinkers, such as Thomas More and Erasmus, advocated for leaders who would serve the greater good and promote the welfare of their communities. This shift from autocratic leadership to a more people-centric approach set the stage for the emergence of servant leadership as a modern leadership philosophy.

In the 20th century, the term "servant leadership" was coined by Robert K. Greenleaf, an executive at AT&T and a prominent management consultant. Greenleaf's groundbreaking essay, "The Servant as Leader," published in 1970, explored the idea of leaders prioritizing their followers' needs rather than their ambitions. Greenleaf's work sparked a paradigm shift in leadership thinking, inspiring CEOs, leaders, and managers to embrace a more servant-oriented approach.

Since then, servant leadership has gained traction in various industries and organizations. It aligns with the changing dynamics of the modern workplace, where employees seek purpose, fulfillment, and a sense of belonging. Servant leaders create a supportive environment that fosters collaboration, trust, and personal growth. They empower their teams, encourage open communication, and actively listen to their employees' concerns and ideas.

The historical background of servant leadership serves as a reminder that leadership is not solely about power and authority. It is about helping others, inspiring excellence, and creating a positive impact on individuals and society as a whole. CEOs, leaders, and managers who embrace servant leadership can cultivate a culture of trust, innovation, and employee engagement, resulting in higher performance and sustainable success.

The historical background of servant leadership illustrates its enduring significance and timeless appeal. From ancient philosophies to modern management theories, servant leadership has transcended time. It inspires CEOs, leaders, and managers to lead with empathy, humility, and a genuine desire to serve others. By understanding its historical roots, leaders can apply the principles of servant leadership in their organizations, thereby inspiring excellence and fostering a culture of collaboration and growth.

The Principles of Servant Leadership

Servant Leadership is a management philosophy that emphasizing serving others first rather than seeking personal gain or power. In this section, we will explore the fundamental principles of Servant Leadership and how they can inspire excellence in CEOs, leaders, and managers across various industries.

1. Putting People First: At the heart of Servant Leadership is the

belief that the needs and well-being of individuals should be the primary focus. Successful leaders prioritize their employees' development, growth, and happiness, creating a positive and supportive work environment.

2. Leading with Empathy: Servant leaders understand the importance of empathy in building solid relationships with their team members. Leaders can foster trust and open communication by actively listening, understanding different perspectives, and showing genuine care and compassion.

3. Building a Collaborative Culture: Servant Leadership promotes collaboration and teamwork. Leaders encourage a culture of inclusivity, where every voice is heard and valued. Leaders can harness their team's collective intelligence and creativity by creating a cooperative environment.

4. Providing Vision and Purpose: Effective leaders inspire their teams by providing a clear vision and purpose. Servant leaders can articulate a compelling vision that aligns with the organization's values, helping employees understand how their contributions contribute to the larger picture.

5. Developing Others: Servant leaders are committed to the growth and development of their employees. They invest in training and mentoring programs, provide opportunities for learning and advancement, and empower individuals to reach their full potential. Leaders enhance the organization's capabilities by developing their team members and building loyalty and engagement.

6. Leading by Example: Servant leaders understand the importance of modeling the behavior they expect from their team. They demonstrate integrity, humility, and a strong work ethic. By leading by example, leaders inspire their employees to follow suit and create a culture of accountability.

7. Servant Leadership in Action: This principle emphasizes the importance of translating theory into practice. Leaders should actively seek opportunities to serve their team members, removing obstacles and providing the necessary resources for success. Leaders can inspire their employees by actively demonstrating servant leadership behaviors and creating a positive and productive workplace.

Servant Leadership is a powerful management philosophy focusing on putting people first, building strong relationships, and fostering a collaborative and purpose-driven culture. By embracing the principles of Servant Leadership, CEOs, leaders, and managers can inspire excellence, drive employee engagement, and achieve long-term success in their organizations.

Chapter 2
The Benefits of Servant Leadership

Improving Employee Engagement and Satisfaction

In business, it has become increasingly evident that a company's success is directly linked to the engagement and satisfaction of its employees. CEOs, leaders, and managers must recognize the importance of fostering a work environment that promotes employee well-being and fulfillment. This section aims to provide valuable insights and practical strategies to enhance employee engagement and satisfaction through the lens of servant leadership.

Servant leadership, as management philosophy prioritizes the needs and development of employees, has gained significant traction in recent years. This approach places the leader in a position of service, actively seeking opportunities to support and empower their team members. By embracing servant leadership principles, CEOs, leaders, and managers can create a culture of trust, collaboration, and shared purpose, ultimately driving employee engagement and satisfaction.

One of the critical aspects of improving employee engagement and satisfaction is ensuring open and effective communication channels. Leaders should actively listen to their employees' concerns, ideas, and feedback, valuing their input and making them feel heard. Regular team meetings, one-on-one check-ins, and anonymous suggestion boxes are just some tools that can facilitate transparent communication.

Furthermore, recognizing and appreciating employees' contributions is crucial for their engagement and satisfaction. Leaders should regularly acknowledge and celebrate individual and team achievements, providing constructive feedback and recognition for a job well done. Implementing a reward and recognition program can also incentivize employees to consistently perform at their best, fostering a positive work environment. Also, promoting continuous learning and development is vital for employee engagement and satisfaction.

The Servant's Leader Playbook:

A Guide to Effective Leadership for All

Leaders should invest in training programs, mentorship opportunities, and career advancement prospects, allowing employees to enhance their skills and reach their full potential. Encouraging an organization's growth mindset can also inspire employee innovation and creativity.

Lastly, CEOs, leaders, and managers need to lead by example. By embodying the values of servant leadership, they can inspire their teams to adopt similar behaviors and attitudes. This includes being approachable, empathetic, supportive and promoting work-life balance and well-being.

Improving employee engagement and satisfaction is critical to effective management and leadership. By embracing servant leadership principles, CEOs, leaders, and managers can create a positive work environment that empowers and motivates their employees. Through open communication, recognition, learning opportunities, and leading by example, organizations can foster a culture of engagement and satisfaction, ultimately driving excellence and success.

Enhancing Team Performance

Effective teamwork is crucial for success in the fast-paced and ever-changing business world. As a CEO, leader, or manager, you are responsible for fostering an environment that enhances team performance. This section will delve into servant leadership and how it can inspire excellence among your team members.

Servant leadership, a philosophy that places the needs of others above one's own, has gained significant traction in recent years. It emphasizes collaboration, empathy, and a focus on team members' development and growth. By adopting this leadership style, you can create a culture that encourages high-performance teams capable of achieving exceptional results.

To enhance team performance, clearly define your team's purpose and goals. Communicate these objectives to your team members and ensure they understand how their efforts contribute to the larger picture. A sense of purpose and alignment will inspire your team to work together towards a common goal.

Empowerment is another crucial element of enhancing team performance. Give your team members the autonomy and authority to make decisions and take ownership of their work. Please encourage them to share their ideas, opinions, and expertise, fostering a sense of ownership and commitment to the team's objectives.

As a servant leader, your role is to provide support and resources to your team members. Identifying their strengths and weaknesses provides the necessary tools and training to help them excel. Offer guidance and mentorship, creating an environment where continuous learning and improvement are valued.

Building trust among team members is imperative for enhanced performance. Foster open and honest communication where everyone feels comfortable sharing their thoughts and concerns. Encourage collaboration and foster a culture of feedback where constructive criticism is welcomed and valued.

Recognize and celebrate the achievements of your team members. Show appreciation for their hard work and dedication. Acknowledge their contributions individually and as a team, and reward their successes. Doing so will motivate your team members to continue striving for excellence. As a CEO, leader, or manager, you have the power to enhance team performance through servant leadership. By fostering a culture of collaboration, empowerment, trust, and recognition, you can inspire excellence among your team members. Embrace the principles of servant leadership, and watch your team achieve remarkable results.

Fostering Positive Organizational Culture

Creating a positive organizational culture is essential for success in today's fast-paced and ever-changing business environment. In this

The Servant's Leader Playbook:

A Guide to Effective Leadership for All

section of "Servant Leadership: Inspiring Excellence in Managers and Executives," we will explore the importance of cultivating a positive culture within your organization and how servant leadership principles can contribute to this goal.

You can shape your organization's culture as a CEO, leader, or manager. A positive culture is where employees feel valued, supported, and motivated to do their best work. It fosters a sense of teamwork, collaboration, and innovation, ultimately leading to increased productivity and employee satisfaction.

Servant leadership is a leadership style that emphasizes the well-being and development of employees. By adopting servant leadership principles, you can create an environment that encourages open communication, trust, and empathy. This, in turn, helps to establish a positive culture within your organization.

One essential aspect of fostering a positive culture is leading by example.

The Servant's Leader Playbook:

A Guide to Effective Leadership for All

As a servant leader, you should embody the values and behaviors you expect from your team. Show empathy and actively listen to your employees' concerns and ideas. Encourage open and honest communication, allowing employees to express their opinions and share feedback. Demonstrating these qualities will inspire your team to do the same, contributing to a positive and collaborative work environment. Additionally, it is crucial to invest in employee development and growth. Provide opportunities for training, mentorship, and advancement. A positive culture supports and encourages personal and professional growth, enabling employees to reach their full potential. Investing in your employees' development enhances their skills and demonstrates your commitment to their success and well-being.

Recognition and appreciation are also powerful tools in fostering a positive culture. Acknowledge the hard work and achievements of your team members regularly. Celebrate milestones and successes, both big and small. Recognizing and appreciating your employees' efforts creates a sense of belonging and motivation, fostering a positive and supportive work environment. Fostering a positive organizational culture is vital for the success of any business. By embracing servant leadership principles, such as leading by example, investing in employee development, and showing recognition and appreciation, you can create a work environment that inspires excellence, collaboration, and innovation. As a CEO, leader, or manager, you are responsible for shaping your organization's culture and creating an atmosphere where employees can thrive and reach their full potential.

Chapter 3
Developing a Servant Leadership Mindset

Cultivating Self-Awareness

In servant leadership, self-awareness is a fundamental trait that distinguishes exceptional CEOs, leaders, and managers from the rest. It is the ability to understand oneself, including strengths, weaknesses, values, and emotions. Cultivating self-awareness enables individuals to lead authentically, make better decisions, and build strong relationships with their teams.

Self-awareness begins with introspection. Taking the time to reflect on one's actions and behaviors allows leaders to gain insight into their motivations and how they impact those around them. By understanding their values and beliefs, leaders can align their actions with their principles, inspiring their teams to do the same. Furthermore, self-awareness enables leaders to identify areas for

Personal growth. By acknowledging their weaknesses and seeking opportunities for improvement, they can lead by example, showing they're teams that continuous learning is essential for success. This openness to personal growth fosters a culture of development within the organization and increases the leader's credibility and effectiveness. Self-awareness also plays a crucial role in emotional intelligence, a vital attribute for servant leaders. Awareness of one's emotions and how they affect others allows leaders to regulate their reactions, remaining calm and composed even in challenging situations. This emotional self-regulation sets the tone for the entire team, promoting a positive and productive work environment.

Moreover, self-awareness enhances empathetic leadership. Understanding one's own emotions enables leaders to empathize with the experiences and feelings of their team members. This empathy fosters trust and collaboration, creating a supportive atmosphere where individuals feel valued and understood.

To cultivate self-awareness, leaders can employ various practices. Regular self-reflection, journaling, and seeking feedback from trusted colleagues or mentors are effective strategies. Mindfulness techniques, such as meditation or deep breathing exercises, can help leaders become more attuned to their thoughts and emotions. Cultivating self-awareness is a vital component of servant leadership. By understanding themselves, leaders can lead authentically, make better decisions, and build strong team relationships. Through introspection, acknowledging weaknesses, and developing emotional intelligence, leaders can inspire excellence and create an environment that fosters growth and collaboration. Embracing self-awareness as an ongoing practice empowers CEOs, leaders, and managers to serve their organizations and teams with integrity and empathy.

Practicing Empathy and Emotional Intelligence

Servant leadership has gained significant traction in today's fast-paced and highly competitive business world. CEOs, leaders, and managers have realized that success lies in serving their teams rather than solely focusing on their achievements. This section, "Practicing Empathy and Emotional Intelligence," delves into the essential qualities of empathy and emotional intelligence and how they can be harnessed to inspire excellence in managers and executives practicing servant leadership.

Empathy, often referred to as the ability to understand and share the feelings of others, is a vital skill for any leader or manager. By cultivating compassion, leaders can foster a culture of trust, collaboration, and mutual respect within their organizations. Empathetic leaders actively listen to their employees, seeking to understand their perspectives and concerns. They demonstrate genuine care and compassion, making their team members feel valued and supported. This, in turn, leads to increased employee engagement, loyalty, and productivity.

On the other hand, emotional intelligence encompasses the ability to recognize, understand, and manage one's emotions and those of others. Leaders with high emotional intelligence are more adept at handling difficult situations, resolving conflicts, and building solid relationships. Servant leaders can effectively motivate and inspire their employees by being in tune with their own emotions and those of their team members, leading to improved performance and overall organizational success.

This section provides practical strategies for CEOs, leaders, and managers to enhance their empathy and emotional intelligence skills. It emphasizes the importance of self-awareness and self-reflection, encouraging leaders to examine their biases and assumptions. It also explores techniques for active listening, such as paraphrasing and asking clarifying questions, which enable leaders to understand the needs and concerns of their team members truly. Additionally, the section delves into the power of non-verbal communication, as a significant portion of communication occurs through body language and facial expressions

Leaders are encouraged to pay attention to these subtle cues and respond appropriately, strengthening their team connection and fostering a positive work environment.

By practicing empathy and emotional intelligence, leaders can create a culture of servant leadership within their organizations. This benefits the individual employees and contributes to the company's overall success and growth. CEOs, leaders, and managers who embrace these qualities will inspire excellence in their teams, unlocking their full potential and achieving sustainable success.

Building Trust and Credibility

In leadership, trust and credibility is the bedrock upon which successful organizations are built. With them, leaders can inspire and motivate their teams, and their organizations will thrive in the face of challenges. This section will delve into building trust and credibility as a servant leader and explore practical strategies to cultivate these vital qualities.

As a CEO, leader, or manager, understanding the concept of servant leadership is crucial. Servant leadership is a philosophy that emphasizes the leader's commitment to serving others, putting their needs and interests first. By adopting this approach, leaders can create an environment of trust and credibility where team members feel valued, supported, and empowered.

Trust is the cornerstone of any successful relationship. It is earned over time through consistent actions and transparent communication. As a servant leader, it is essential to lead by example and demonstrate integrity in all interactions. This means keeping promises, admitting mistakes, and being accountable for actions. By doing so, leaders can build trust with their team members, fostering an environment where open dialogue and collaboration thrive.

Credibility is closely linked to trust. It is the perception of a leader's competence, character, and values. To establish credibility, leaders must continuously develop their skills and expertise. This can be achieved through ongoing learning, seeking feedback, and staying abreast of industry trends. Additionally, leaders must align their actions with their stated values, as inconsistencies erode credibility. By being authentic to themselves, leaders can inspire confidence and gain the respect of their team members.

Servant leaders must also prioritize effective communication to foster trust and credibility within an organization. Transparent and open communication builds trust by ensuring that team members are well-informed, included, and have a voice in decision-making processes. Leaders should actively listen to their team members' concerns, provide regular feedback, and encourage open dialogue. By doing so, leaders demonstrate their commitment to their teams' growth and well-being, further enhancing trust and credibility.

Building trust and credibility is paramount for CEOs, leaders, and managers practicing servant leadership. By embodying the principles of servant leadership, leaders can create an environment where trust thrives, fostering collaboration and innovation. Through consistent actions, transparent communication, and a commitment to personal growth, leaders can establish their credibility and inspire excellence in their teams. By investing in trust and credibility, leaders lay the foundation for long-term success and create a servant leadership culture that permeates the organization.

Chapter 4
Leading by Example

Setting Clear Goals and Expectations

As a CEO, leader, or manager, one of the most crucial aspects of your role is to set clear goals and expectations for your team. In the realm of servant leadership, this becomes even more vital as it fosters an environment of trust, collaboration, and excellence. By clearly defining goals and expectations, you empower your team members to perform at their best and align their efforts with the organization's vision.

When setting goals, it is imperative to ensure they are SMART (Specific, Measurable, Achievable, Relevant, and Time-bound). Specific objectives provide clarity and direction, while measurable goals allow tracking progress and evaluating success. Achievable goals are realistic and attainable, preventing frustration or demotivation. Relevant goals align with the organization's mission and vision, contributing to its success. Lastly, time-bound goals establish clear deadlines, promoting accountability and a sense of urgency.

In addition to setting SMART goals, it is equally important to communicate clear expectations to your team members. Expectations should encompass performance standards, behavior, and the desired outcome. By explicitly stating what you expect from your team members, you eliminate ambiguity and create a foundation for success. Remember to make these expectations realistic, fair, and transparent, ensuring everyone understands their requirements.

Involving your team in the process is vital to set goals and expectations effectively. Encourage open communication and active participation, allowing team members to provide input and share their perspectives. Applying them creates a sense of ownership and commitment, motivating them to strive for excellence. Moreover, consider tailoring goals and expectations to individual strengths and aspirations, as this will empower team members and enable them to contribute their best work.

Furthermore, continuously evaluate and provide feedback on progress towards goals and expectations. Regular check-ins and performance reviews allow for course correction, recognition of achievements, and identification of areas for improvement. This feedback loop ensures accountability and strengthens the relationship between leaders and team members, fostering a culture of continuous learning and growth,

Setting clear goals and expectations is fundamental to servant leadership. By utilizing SMART goals, involving your team in the process, and providing regular feedback, you create an environment that inspires excellence and promotes collaboration. As a CEO, leader, or manager, you guide your team toward success by setting clear goals and expectations that align with the organization's vision.

Communicating Effectively

Effective communication has become indispensable for CEOs, leaders, and managers in today's fast-paced and rapidly changing business landscape. In servant leadership, communication is vital in inspiring excellence and fostering a culture of collaboration and trust within organizations. This section delves into the significance of effective communication in the context of servant leadership, providing actionable tips and strategies for enhancing communication skills.

Unlike traditional leadership styles, servant leadership prioritizes employees' needs and aims to empower them to reach their full potential. Central to this approach is the ability to communicate effectively, enabling leaders to build meaningful connections with their teams. By fostering open and honest communication channels, servant leaders create a safe space where employees feel valued and heard. This, in turn, boosts morale, engagement, and productivity.

One of the critical aspects of effective communication in servant

34

The Servant's Leader Playbook:
A Guide to Effective Leadership for All

leadership is active listening. Leaders must listen attentively to their employees, demonstrating empathy and understanding. By actively engaging in conversations and seeking to comprehend the perspectives of others, leaders can build trust and foster a culture of inclusivity. Additionally, active listening helps identify and address employees' concerns or challenges, promoting a supportive work environment.

Another crucial component of effective communication is clarity. Servant leaders must be able to articulate their vision, goals, and expectations clearly, ensuring that employees understand their roles and responsibilities. By providing concise and transparent communication, leaders empower their teams to make informed decisions and take ownership of their work. Clear communication also helps avoid misunderstandings and conflicts, promoting a harmonious and productive workplace.

Furthermore, servant leaders should embrace various communication channels to cater to the diverse needs of their employees. Whether face-to-face meetings, email, or virtual platforms, choosing the appropriate medium is essential for effective communication. Leaders must also adapt their communication style to accommodate different personalities and communication preferences, fostering effective collaboration and understanding. Effective communication lies at the core of servant leadership, inspiring excellence in managers and executives. Servant leaders can create a culture of trust, collaboration, and empowerment by actively listening, practicing clarity, and utilizing diverse communication channels. Embracing these strategies will enhance communication skills, strengthen relationships, drive employee engagement, and ultimately contribute to the organization's overall success.

.

Demonstrating Integrity and Ethic

In today's fast-paced business environment, where competition is fierce and profit margins are often the ultimate goal, CEOs, leaders, and managers must embrace the principles of integrity and ethics. In servant leadership, these values are desirable and essential for creating a culture of excellence and inspiring greatness in teams and organizations.

Integrity forms the foundation of servant leadership. It is the unwavering commitment to doing what is right, even when faced with difficult choices or tempting shortcuts. As a CEO, leader, or manager, your actions and decisions set the tone for your organization. Demonstrating integrity in all aspects of your leadership inspires trust and builds credibility with your team and stakeholders, customers, and the wider community.

Ethics, on the other hand, go beyond mere compliance with laws and regulations. Servant leaders understand that ethics are about doing what is morally right, even when it may not be the most profitable or convenient choice. Upholding ethical standards and values ensures fair treatment, transparency, and accountability within your organization. It fosters a culture of respect and empowers employees to make moral decisions themselves, aligning their actions with the organization's overarching goals.

Demonstrating integrity and ethics as a servant leader involves leading by example. Your actions must consistently align with your words, setting a high standard for others to follow. Communicate your values clearly and consistently, and hold yourself and others accountable for upholding them. Actively seek opportunities to reinforce integrity and ethics within your organization through training programs, policies, and regular communication. Encourage open dialogue and provide channels for reporting ethical concerns without fear of retaliation.

Servant leaders also recognize the importance of self-reflection and continuous improvement. Regularly assess your actions and decisions, seeking feedback from your team and other stakeholders. Embrace transparency and learn from your mistakes, demonstrating humility and a willingness to grow and adapt. By embodying integrity and ethical behavior, you inspire trust, foster a sense of purpose, and make a lasting impact on your organization and its stakeholders. Serve as a role model, communicate your values, and embrace self-improvement to inspire excellence in those you lead truly.

Chapter 5
Empowering Others

Delegating Authority and Responsibility

In servant leadership, one of the essential skills for CEOs, leaders, and managers to master is the art of delegating authority and responsibility. Delegation is not merely assigning tasks to subordinates; it involves a thoughtful and strategic approach to empower and inspire team members, fostering their growth and development while achieving organizational goals.

Delegating authority is about entrusting individuals with decision-making power and the ability to act on behalf of the organization. By empowering employees, leaders create a culture of ownership and accountability where individuals feel valued and motivated to contribute their best. This practice lets leaders focus on higher-level strategic initiatives, knowing their teams can handle day-to-day operations.

However, delegating authority should always be accompanied by delegating responsibility. Leaders must clearly define the scope and expectations of the delegated task, ensuring that team members understand their roles and the desired outcomes. This clarity not only prevents misunderstandings but also enables employees to take ownership of their responsibilities and make informed decisions in alignment with the organization's values and objectives.

Delegation is not a one-size-fits-all approach; it requires leaders to assess individual strengths, weaknesses, and developmental needs. By matching tasks to employees' skill sets, leaders can maximize their team's potential and foster a sense of pride and accomplishment. Additionally, leaders should provide the necessary support, resources, and guidance to ensure success while also allowing room for autonomy and creative problem-solving.

Effective delegation promotes a culture of collaboration and trust within the organization. It encourages open communication, as team members feel comfortable seeking guidance or sharing ideas, knowing their input is valued. Furthermore, it fosters a learning environment where employees can develop new skills, gain experience, and grow professionally.

However, leaders must also be cautious to avoid over-delegating or under-delegating. Over-delegating can overwhelm team members, leading to burnout and a decline in performance. On the other hand, under-delegating can hinder employee growth and limit the organization's potential for innovation and adaptability. Delegation is a vital aspect of servant leadership that empowers individuals promotes accountability, and enhances organizational effectiveness. CEOs, leaders, and managers must recognize the value of delegating authority and responsibility, as it benefits the organization and fosters employee growth and satisfaction. By mastering the art of delegation, leaders can inspire excellence, build stronger teams, and ultimately achieve tremendous success in servant leadership.

Encouraging Creativity and Innovation

Creativity and innovation have become crucial for success in today's rapidly changing business landscape. As a CEO, leader, or manager, you are responsible for fostering a culture that encourages and nurtures these qualities within your organization. This

section will explore the significance of creativity and innovation in the context of servant leadership and provide practical strategies to inspire excellence in your team.

Servant leadership emphasizes serving others and empowering them to reach their full potential. Encouraging creativity and innovation aligns perfectly with this philosophy, as it involves empowering individuals to think outside the box, take risks, and challenge the status quo.

Creating a safe and supportive environment is essential to cultivate creativity and innovation within your team. Foster open communication channels where team members feel comfortable sharing their ideas, thoughts, and concerns. Listen to their input and validate their contributions, even if they must align with your initial vision. Emphasize the value of diverse perspectives and encourage collaboration across different departments and hierarchical levels.

Furthermore, as a servant leader, providing resources and opportunities for professional development is crucial. Invest in training programs, workshops, and conferences on creativity and innovation. Encourage your team members to explore their passions and interests, even if they may seem unrelated to their current roles. By facilitating a continuous learning environment, you empower individuals to think creatively and apply innovative approaches to problem-solving.

Recognize and reward creative thinking and innovative solutions. Acknowledge and celebrate the achievements of individuals and teams who challenge the status quo and develop groundbreaking ideas. Doing so reinforces your organization's importance of creativity and innovation and inspires others to follow suit.

Lastly, as a servant leader, it is crucial to lead by example. Demonstrate your commitment to creativity and innovation through your actions and decisions. Encourage calculated risk-taking and embrace failure as an opportunity for growth and learning. By showing vulnerability and resilience, you create a culture that supports experimentation and fosters a growth mindset.

Encouraging creativity and innovation is essential to servant leadership. By creating a safe and supportive environment, providing resources for professional development, recognizing and rewarding creative thinking, and leading by example, you inspire excellence within your organization. Embrace the power of creativity and innovation, and watch your team and business thrive in the face of evolving challenges.

Supporting Professional Growth and Development

Supporting professional growth and development has become crucial for CEOs, leaders, and managers. As advocates of servant leadership, we must embrace the responsibility of nurturing the potential of our employees and creating an environment that fosters continuous learning and growth. Professional growth and development go hand in hand with servant leadership principles. By prioritizing the development of our team members, we demonstrate our commitment to their success and well-being. Servant leaders understand that investing in their employees' growth benefits the individual and contributes to the organization's success.

One of the key ways to support professional growth and development is by providing opportunities for learning and skill enhancement. This can include workshops, seminars, conferences, and mentorship programs. By offering these avenues, we empower our employees to expand their knowledge, acquire new skills, and stay updated with industry trends. Additionally, providing access to formal education or professional certifications can help individuals reach their full potential and contribute more effectively to the organization.

Another critical aspect of supporting professional growth is creating a culture encouraging learning and personal development. As leaders, we must foster an environment where curiosity, experimentation and continuous improvement are celebrated. Encouraging employees to take risks, learn from failures, and share their knowledge with others helps create a dynamic and innovative workplace. Additionally, regular performance evaluations and constructive feedback are essential in supporting professional growth. Providing clear and specific feedback enables individuals to identify improvement areas and set development goals. Offering coaching and mentoring to employees can further enhance their growth by providing guidance and support tailored to their unique needs. Promoting a healthy work-life balance is crucial for professional growth and development. Encouraging employees to harmonize their personal and professional lives enhances their well-being and boosts their productivity and motivation. Offering flexible work arrangements and wellness programs and promoting self-care initiatives can support this balance. As CEOs, leaders, and managers, we are responsible for supporting our employees' professional growth and development. By embracing servant leadership principles and creating an environment that prioritizes learning, feedback, and work-life balance, we can inspire excellence and cultivate a culture of continuous growth within our organization. When we invest in our employees' development, we invest in the success and future of our organization as well.

Chapter 6
Serving the Team

Creating a Supportive and Inclusive Environment

In today's business landscape, it is becoming increasingly important for organizations to cultivate a supportive and inclusive environment. This section will delve into the significance of creating such an environment and how servant leadership can be instrumental in achieving it. CEOs, leaders, and managers will find valuable insights and practical strategies to foster a culture of support and inclusivity within their organizations.

A supportive and inclusive environment is not just a buzzword; it is the foundation for high-performing teams and a thriving organizational culture. Employees who feel supported and included are more engaged, motivated, and productive. This translates into better business outcomes and a competitive edge. The role of servant leadership in creating this environment cannot be overstated. Servant leadership is a leadership philosophy that emphasizes the well-being and growth of employees. It is about leading with empathy, humility, and a deep commitment to serving others. By practicing servant leadership, CEOs, leaders, and managers can create an environment where everyone feels valued, heard, and empowered. This section will explore various servant leadership practices that can be implemented to foster a supportive and inclusive environment.

One such practice is active listening. Leaders who genuinely listen to their employees without judgment or interruption create a safe space for open communication and collaboration. This enables individuals to share their unique perspectives, ideas, and concerns, leading to more innovative and inclusive decision-making. Another critical aspect of creating a supportive and inclusive environment is providing opportunities for growth and development. Servant leaders prioritize the growth and development of their employees, recognizing that investing in their skills and abilities benefits the individuals and the organization as a whole. This section will discuss strategies for fostering a learning culture and providing mentorship and coaching opportunities.

Additionally, this section will examine the significance of fostering diversity and inclusion within the organization. Servant leaders understand that diversity encompasses more than race and gender; it includes a variety of thoughts, backgrounds, and experiences. By embracing diversity and promoting inclusivity, leaders can tap into the collective intelligence of their teams, resulting in better decision-making and problem-solving. Creating a supportive and inclusive environment is crucial for organizational success in today's complex business landscape. Servant leadership provides a framework for CEOs, leaders, and managers to cultivate such an environment by practicing active listening, prioritizing employee growth and development, and fostering diversity and inclusion. By embracing these principles, leaders can inspire excellence in their teams and drive organizational success.

Resolving Conflicts and Nurturing Collaboration

Conflicts will arise within teams and organizations in the fast-paced and competitive business world. As CEO, leaders, and managers, it is essential to understand the importance of resolving disputes and nurturing collaboration to create a positive work environment and drive excellence. This section will delve into the principles of servant leadership and how they can be applied to resolve conflicts and foster collaboration within teams effectively.

Servant leadership is a leadership philosophy that prioritizes the needs of others and focuses on serving the organization's greater good. It emphasizes empathy, active listening, and open communication, which are crucial when dealing with conflicts. By adopting a servant leadershi mindset, CEOs, leaders, and managers can create a safe space for employees to voice their concerns and address disputes constructively.

The Servant's Leader Playbook:

A Guide to Effective Leadership for All

One of the critical strategies for resolving conflicts is encouraging open dialogue and active listening. Servant leaders take the time to understand each individual's perspective, allowing them to identify the root causes of conflicts and find win-win solutions. By promoting open communication channels, leaders can ensure that disputes are addressed promptly and effectively, preventing them from escalating and negatively impacting the team's dynamics.

Furthermore, servant leaders foster collaboration by creating an inclusive and supportive work environment. They actively encourage teamwork, promote diversity, and value each team member's contributions. By leveraging every individual's unique strengths and skills, servant leaders nurture collaboration and create a sense of unity among team members. This collaborative mindset leads to increased creativity, improved problem-solving abilities, and higher employee engagement.

In addition, servant leaders also play a crucial role in mediating conflicts and facilitating productive discussions. They act as neutral mediators, guiding the conversation toward a solution that satisfies all parties involved. Servant leaders promote fairness and ensure that all voices are heard by remaining impartial and objective.

Resolving conflicts and nurturing collaboration is not a one-time task but an ongoing process. It requires continuous effort and commitment from CEOs, leaders, and managers. Adopting the principles of servant leadership can create a culture of trust, respect, and collaboration, ultimately leading to higher employee satisfaction, increased productivity, and long-term organizational success. This section highlights the importance of resolving conflicts and nurturing cooperation in the context of servant leadership. CEOs, leaders, and managers can benefit from implementing these principles to create a harmonious work environment and inspire excellence within their teams. They can build solid, cohesive groups that drive success by prioritizing open communication, active listening, and inclusive collaboration.

Recognizing and Celebrating Achievements

Leaders and managers must recognize and celebrate their teams' achievements. Doing so boosts employee morale and fosters a culture of excellence and servant leadership. This section will explore the importance of recognizing achievements and provide practical strategies for effectively celebrating accomplishments.

Servant leaders understand that their success is directly linked to the success of their teams. They recognize that each individual's contribution is valuable and essential to achieving organizational goals. By acknowledging and celebrating achievements, leaders show appreciation for their employees' hard work, dedication, and commitment. This recognition motivates employees to continue performing at their best and fosters a sense of loyalty and engagement.

Celebrating achievements is not limited to significant milestones or extraordinary accomplishments. Servant leaders understand the power of recognizing even the most minor wins. Leaders create a positive and supportive work environment by celebrating incremental progress and small victories. This culture of celebration encourages employees to strive for excellence and fosters a sense of camaraderie and teamwork.

Leaders can utilize several effective strategies to recognize and celebrate achievements. One such strategy is public recognition. By publicly acknowledging an employee's accomplishments, leaders make the individual feel valued and inspire others to strive for similar success. This can be done through team meetings, company-wide emails, or even in front of clients or stakeholders.

Another powerful strategy is offering rewards and incentives. Whether it is a monetary bonus, a promotion, or a simple token of appreciation tangible rewards can motivate employees and reinforce their commitment to excellence. Leaders can also consider organizing celebratory events such as team lunches, outings, or annual awards ceremonies to recognize outstanding achievements. Leaders should also encourage peer-to-peer recognition. Leaders foster a culture of support and collaboration by empowering employees to acknowledge and celebrate each other's accomplishments. This strengthens the bond between team members and creates a sense of shared responsibility for the organization's success. Recognizing and celebrating achievements is fundamental to servant leadership. By actively acknowledging and appreciating the efforts and accomplishments of their teams, leaders inspire excellence, foster a positive work culture, and motivate employees to continue striving for success. By implementing public recognition, offering rewards, and encouraging peer-to-peer recognition, leaders can create a work environment that celebrates accomplishments and inspires continuous growth and improvement.

Chapter 7
Servant Leadership in Practice

Applying Servant Leadership in Decision-Making

In leadership, decision-making plays a crucial role in shaping the direction and success of organizations. However, traditional leadership models often prioritize leaders' authority and decision-making power, which can lead to a lack of employee engagement and limited creativity in problem-solving. This is where the concept of Servant Leadership comes into play.

Servant Leadership is a transformative approach and a philosophy that encourages leaders to see themselves as servants to their teams and stakeholders rather than dictators. By adopting this mindset, leaders can foster a culture of trust, openness, and innovation, leading to better decision-making processes and outcomes. In applying Servant Leadership principles to decision-making, CEOs,

The Servant's Leader Playbook:

A Guide to Effective Leadership for All

eaders, and managers can create an environment that encourages

participation, diversity of ideas, and shared ownership. By actively

nvolving team members in the decision-making process, leaders can

ap into the collective wisdom and expertise of the entire

organization, making better-informed decisions that consider a

broader range of perspectives.

One key aspect of applying Servant Leadership in decision-making is

he ability to listen actively. By attentively listening to team members'

opinions, concerns, and suggestions, leaders can create an inclusive

environment where everyone feels heard and valued. This not only

boosts employee morale but also enhances the quality of decisions by

incorporating a variety of viewpoints. Additionally, Servant

Leadership encourages leaders to empower their teams to make

decisions autonomously whenever possible. Leaders can foster a sense

of ownership and accountability among team members by delegating

decision-making responsibilities and providing the necessary support and resources. This increases their engagement and leads to more creative and innovative solutions. Also, Servant Leadership emphasizes ethical decision-making. Leaders are encouraged to consider the long-term impact of their decisions on all stakeholders, including employees, customers, and the community. This holistic perspective ensures that decisions are made with integrity and align with the organization's values and purpose.

Applying Servant Leadership in decision-making can profoundly impact the effectiveness and success of organizations. By prioritizing collaboration, empathy, and empowerment, leaders can create a culture that values team members' input and harnesses their collective wisdom. This approach leads to better decision-making processes, increased employee engagement, and, ultimately, excellence in managerial and executive roles.

Implementing Servant Leadership in Change Management

The Servant's Leader Playbook:

A Guide to Effective Leadership for All

Change is an inevitable part of any organization's growth and development. However, managing change effectively can be daunting for CEOs, leaders, and managers. Traditional hierarchical leadership approaches often need to improve in dealing with the complexities and challenges of change. This is where the concept of servant leadership comes into play.

Servant leadership, a philosophy coined by Robert K. Greenleaf, places the needs of others before self-interest. It focuses on empowering and serving the people within an organization rather than relying on authority and control. By implementing servant leadership principles in change management, CEOs, leaders, and managers can create a culture of trust, collaboration, and innovation, enabling their organizations to thrive in times of change. One of the fundamental aspects of servant leadership in change management is the emphasis on listening and understanding.

The Servant's Leader Playbook:

A Guide to Effective Leadership for All

By actively listening to employees' concerns, ideas, and feedback, leaders can gain valuable insights into the challenges and opportunities associated with change. This creates a sense of psychological safety and encourages open communication, fostering a collaborative environment where everyone's voice is heard and valued.

Furthermore, servant leadership encourages leaders to be empathetic and supportive. Change can be unsettling for employees, causing resistance and anxiety. By demonstrating empathy and providing support, leaders can help their teams navigate the uncertainties of change. This can be achieved through coaching, mentoring, and ensuring employees have the necessary resources and training to adapt and succeed in the new environment.

Another crucial aspect of implementing servant leadership in change management is the focus on developing and empowering employees. Servant leaders believe in the potential of their team members and ctively work toward their growth and development. This involves providing learning opportunities, fostering a culture of continuous improvement, and delegating responsibilities to encourage autonomy and ownership. By empowering employees, leaders enhance their skills and capabilities and create a sense of right and commitment toward the change initiative; implementing servant leadership in change management can be transformative for CEOs, leaders, and managers. Organizations can navigate change more effectively by prioritizing employees' needs, fostering trust and collaboration, and empowering individuals. Servant leadership enables leaders to create an environment where employees feel valued, supported, and inspired to embrace change and contribute their best to organizational success.

Overcoming Challenges and Sustaining Servant Leadership

Servant leadership is a powerful and transformative leadership philosophy that has the potential to revolutionize organizations. However, implementing and sustaining servant leadership can face its

The Servant's Leader Playbook:

A Guide to Effective Leadership for All

fair share of challenges. In this section, we will explore some of the common obstacles CEOs, leaders, and managers face on their journey toward becoming servant leaders and provide practical strategies for overcoming these challenges and sustaining servant leadership within their organizations.

One of the biggest challenges in adopting servant leadership is the resistance and skepticism that may arise within the organization. Traditional leadership models often emphasize authority and control, while servant leadership focuses on empowering others and serving their needs. This paradigm shift can be met with resistance, as some employees may need clarification about the intentions behind this leadership style. To overcome this challenge, CEOs, leaders, and managers must lead by example and demonstrate servant leadership's positive impact on individual and organizational performance. By consistently embodying servant leadership principles and showcasing their benefits, leaders can gradually win over the hearts and minds of their teams.

Another challenge in sustaining servant leadership is the temptation to revert to old habits and practices. It is easy to fall back into a command-and-control style of leadership during times of crisis or when faced with tough decisions. However, true servant leaders understand the importance of staying true to their values and principles, even in challenging situations. By constantly reminding themselves of their purpose and seeking feedback from the team members, leaders can visit grounded and maintain their servant leadership mindset.

Furthermore, servant leadership requires a shift in mindset from a short-term focus to a long-term perspective. This can be challenging for leaders accustomed to immediate results and quick fixes. Servant leadership is a journey, not a destination, requiring patience, perseverance, and a commitment to continuous improvement. Leaders must resist the urge to prioritize short-term gains over the long-term well-being of their employees and the organization.

Finally, sustaining servant leadership requires building a culture that supports and reinforces these values. This involves aligning organizational systems, processes, and practices with servant leadership principles. From performance evaluations to recruitment and selection, every aspect of the organization should reflect and promote servant leadership. CEOs, leaders, and managers must also invest in ongoing training and development to ensure that employees at all levels understand and embrace the servant leadership philosophy. While becoming a servant leader may be challenging, the rewards are well worth the effort. By overcoming resistance, staying true to their values, adopting a long-term perspective, and building a culture that supports servant leadership, CEOs, leaders, and managers can create thriving organizations that inspire excellence and bring out the best in their employees.

Chapter 8
Measuring Succes Servant Leadership

Assessing Employee Satisfaction and Engagement

In servant leadership, one of the primary goals for CEOs, leaders, and managers is to create a work environment that fosters employee satisfaction and engagement. Recognizing the importance of this aspect is crucial, as it directly impacts productivity, retention rates, and overall organizational success. Therefore, it becomes imperative for leaders to assess employee satisfaction and engagement levels within their teams regularly.

Measuring employee satisfaction and engagement requires a multi-faceted approach. Traditional methods like surveys and questionnaires can provide valuable insights into employees' happiness and commitment. These tools gauge work-life balance, job security, growth opportunities, and recognition. Additionally, open and transparent communication channels should be established to encourage employees to share their concerns, ideas, and feedback freely. However, assessing employee satisfaction and engagement goes beyond just collecting data. It requires a genuine commitment from leaders to actively listen and respond to the needs and concerns of their employees. By adopting a servant leadership mindset, leaders can create an inclusive and supportive culture that empowers individuals to thrive.

To effectively assess employee satisfaction and engagement, leaders should consider implementing regular one-on-one meetings with their team members. These meetings serve as

The Servant's Leader Playbook:

A Guide to Effective Leadership for All

a platform for employees to express their thoughts, ambitions, and challenges. Leaders should actively listen, provide constructive feedback, and offer support to help employees overcome obstacles and achieve their goals.

Leaders should encourage collaboration and teamwork, as these factors play a significant role in fostering a sense of belonging and engagement. Creating cross-functional projects, organizing team-building activities, and recognizing collective achievements can strengthen the bond between employees and enhance their overall job satisfaction.

By consistently assessing employee satisfaction and engagement, leaders can identify areas of improvement and implement targeted strategies to enhance the work experience for their teams. Prioritizing employee well-being, recognizing individual contributions, and promoting a healthy work-life balance are all critical components of servant leadership. Assessing employee satisfaction and engagement is crucial to servant leadership. By regularly evaluating the happiness and commitment of employees, leaders can create a positive work environment that fosters growth, productivity, and success. Through open communication, active listening, and a commitment to employee well-being, leaders can inspire excellence within their organizations and cultivate a culture of servant leadership.

Evaluating Team Performance and Productivity

Introduction:

Empowering and inspiring teams to achieve excellence is of paramount importance. However, as a CEO, leader, or manager, it is equally essential to evaluate team performance and productivity to ensure the organization's success. This section delves into the critical aspects of evaluating team performance and productivity and provides valuable insights to help you harness the true potential of servant leadership within your organization.

Setting Clear Expectations:

To evaluate team performance effectively, it is crucial to establish clear expectations from the start. Clearly defining goals, objectives, and performance metrics provides a framework for assessing team performance. By aligning these expectations with the organization's overarching mission and vision, servant leaders can ensure that every team member comprehends their role and responsibilities, fostering a sense of purpose and accountability.

The Servant's Leader Playbook:

A Guide to Effective Leadership for All

Providing Regular Feedback:

Servant leaders understand the significance of ongoing feedback in enhancing team performance. Regular feedback sessions enable leaders to recognize individual and collective achievements, address concerns, and guide improvement. By creating an environment that fosters open communication and constructive feedback, servant leaders encourage continuous growth and development within their teams.

Implementing Performance Measurement Tools:

Incorporating performance measurement tools is instrumental in evaluating team productivity. Managers can objectively assess individual and team performance using key performance indicators (KPIs). These tools enable servant leaders to identify areas of strength, areas for improvement and track progress over time. Additionally, performance measurement tools provide valuable insights to make informed decisions and allocate resources effectively.

Recognizing and Rewarding Excellence:
Servant leaders understand the importance of acknowledging and rewarding excellence within their teams. Celebrating individual and collective achievements boosts morale and motivates team members to perform at their best. By implementing recognition programs, such as employee of the month or team awards, servant leaders create a culture of appreciation and inspire their teams to strive for excellence consistently.

Continuous Learning and Development:
Evaluating team performance and productivity goes hand in hand with promoting continuous learning and development. Servant leaders encourage their teams to acquire new skills,

expand their knowledge, and stay updated with industry trends. By fostering a learning culture, leaders can enhance team performance and productivity while nurturing personal and professional growth within their team members.

Conclusion:

Evaluating team performance and productivity is an essential aspect of servant leadership. By setting clear expectations, providing regular feedback, implementing performance measurement tools, recognizing and rewarding excellence, and promoting continuous learning and development, CEO, leaders, and managers can inspire and empower their teams to achieve excellence. Embracing servant leadership principles and effectively evaluating team performance will drive organizational success and cultivate a culture of trust, collaboration, and continuous improvement.

Tracking Long-Term Organized Growth and Success

CEOs, leaders, and managers constantly seek ways to drive long-term organizational growth and ensure sustained success. One of the most effective approaches to achieving this is through the practice of servant leadership. This section will explore the importance of tracking long-term growth and success and how servant leadership can inspire excellence in managers and executives.

Successful organizations understand the significance of tracking progress and setting goals to measure their long-term growth. By establishing key performance indicators (KPIs) aligned with the company's vision and mission, leaders can monitor the organization's overall health and identify areas for improvement. Servant leaders take this further by focusing on financial metrics and evaluating their impact on employees, customers, and the more significant ones.

Community:

A crucial aspect of tracking long-term growth is fostering a culture of open communication and accountability. Servant leaders create an environment where team members feel empowered to voice their ideas, concerns, and challenges. By encouraging feedback and actively listening to their employees, leaders can identify potential roadblocks to growth and address them proactively. This open dialogue also helps align individual and team goals with the organization's strategic objectives, ensuring everyone is working towards the same vision.

The Servant's Leader Playbook:

A Guide to Effective Leadership for All

Furthermore, servant leadership emphasizes the importance of employee development and engagement. Leaders who prioritize the growth and well-being of their employees create a workforce that is motivated, loyal, and committed to the organization's success. By investing in training programs, mentorship opportunities, and performance evaluations, managers can track their employees' progress and identify areas where additional support or resources may be required.

Servant leaders also embrace innovation and adaptability to effectively track long-term growth and success. They encourage experimentation, embrace failure as a learning opportunity, and continuously seek ways to improve processes and products. By staying ahead of industry trends and anticipating future challenges, leaders can make informed decisions that drive growth and ensure the organization's long-term success. Tracking long-term organizational change and success is essential to servant leadership. By setting measurable goals, fostering open communication, prioritizing employee development, and embracing innovation, managers and executives can inspire excellence within their organizations. Servant leadership provides a framework that not only focuses on financial metrics but also on the well-being of employees and the impact on the larger community. By practicing servant leadership principles, CEOs, leaders, and managers can create a thriving organization that achieves sustained success in today's dynamic business landscape.

Chapter 9
Developing Future Servant Leadership

Mentoring and Coaching Potential Leaders

In the ever-changing business world, CEOs, leaders, and managers must cultivate a new generation of leaders who can navigate future challenges. One of the most effective ways to achieve this is through servant leadership, which emphasizes the development and empowerment of individuals within an organization. Mentoring and coaching potential leader is an essential aspect of servant leadership. It involves taking the time to identify employees with high potential and offering guidance and support to help them grow and excel in their roles. By investing in the development of these individuals, servant leaders not only nurture their talents but also create a culture of continuous improvement and innovation.

The Servant's Leader Playbook:

A Guide to Effective Leadership for All

When mentoring and coaching potential leaders, CEOs, leaders, and managers need to adopt a servant mindset; this means putting the needs and growth of their mentees first rather than focusing solely on their success. Doing so creates an environment of trust and collaboration where potential leaders feel valued and supported.

Effective mentoring and coaching require a deep understanding of each individual's strengths, weaknesses, and aspirations. Servant leaders should take the time to have meaningful conversations with their mentees to gain insights into their motivations and goals. This knowledge can tailor the coaching process and provide targeted guidance and feedback. Mentoring and coaching potential leaders should be a holistic process beyond technical skills. Servant leaders should also focus on developing their mentees' emotional

The Servant's Leader Playbook:

A Guide to Effective Leadership for All

intelligence, communication abilities, and critical thinking skills. By nurturing these qualities, potential leaders will be better equipped to handle the complexities of leadership and inspire excellence in their teams.

Furthermore, servant leaders should encourage potential leaders to take on new challenges and stretch their capabilities. This can be achieved by providing growth opportunities like special projects or cross-functional collaborations. Servant leaders help them build resilience and develop a growth mindset by pushing their mentees out of their comfort zones. Mentoring and coaching potential leaders is crucial to servant leadership. By investing time and effort into developing individuals with high potential, CEOs, leaders, and managers create a pipeline of capable leaders who can drive excellence within their organizations. Through a servant mindset, understanding each individual's strengths and weaknesses, and fostering personal and professional growth, these potential leaders can be empowered to reach their full potential and inspire excellence in others.

Creating Leadership Development Programs

In today's fast-paced and ever-changing business landscape, organizations realize the significance of strong leadership at all levels. As a CEO, leader, or manager, you play a crucial role in shaping your company's future and guiding your team toward success. To truly inspire excellence and foster a culture of servant leadership within your organization, it is essential to implement effective leadership development programs.

The Servant's Leader Playbook:

A Guide to Effective Leadership for All

Leadership development programs are designed to identify and nurture potential leaders, enhance their skills, and equip them with the tools they need to lead excellently. By investing in the growth and development of your employees, you not only create a pipeline of capable leaders and demonstrate your commitment to their long-term success and well-being.

When creating leadership development programs, it is essential to align them with the principles of servant leadership. Servant leadership is a leadership philosophy that emphasizes serving others as the primary objective of leadership. By focusing on the needs of your team members, empowering them, and fostering a sense of community and collaboration, servant leadership creates a positive and inclusive work environment that drives growth and innovation. To create a leadership development program, identify the core competencies and skills required for effective leadership within your organization. These may include communication, decision-making, emotional intelligence, strategic thinking, and adaptability. Once you have identified these competencies, you can design training modules, workshops, and mentoring programs that address these specific areas.

In addition to formal training, providing opportunities for practical application and experiential learning is essential. This can include assigning leadership roles on projects, cross-functional team collaborations, or even organizing community service initiatives. Encouraging leaders to step outside their comfort zones and take calculated risks will help them develop confidence, resilience, and problem-solving abilities. Incorporating coaching and mentorship into your leadership development program can provide invaluable guidance and support. Pairing emerging leaders with experienced mentors allows for knowledge transfer, development of leadership skills, and personal growth.

Lastly, regularly evaluating and reassessing the effectiveness of your leadership development program is crucial. Solicit participant feedback, track their progress, and make necessary adjustments to ensure continuous improvement. By creating leadership development programs that embrace servant leadership principles, you develop strong leaders and foster a culture of excellence, collaboration, and employee engagement. Investing in your employee's growth and development is a win-win situation that will drive the long-term success of your organization.

Instilling Servant Leadership Philosophy in the Organization

As discussed, Servant Leadership has emerged as a powerful and transformative leadership style that has the potential to create a positive impact on organizations and their stakeholders. This section will explore how CEOs, leaders, and managers can instill the Servant Leadership philosophy in their organizations to inspire excellence and drive sustainable success.

At its core, Servant Leadership is about flipping the traditional leadership model on its head. Instead of leaders being at the top and employees at the bottom, Servant Leadership places the leader in a position of service to their team members. This philosophy emphasizes the importance of putting the needs of others first, fostering a culture of collaboration, empathy, and trust.

The Servant's Leader Playbook:

A Guide to Effective Leadership for All

CEOs, leaders, and managers must lead by example to instill the Servant Leadership philosophy in the organization. They must embody the values and principles of Servant Leadership in their daily actions and decision-making processes. By demonstrating humility, empathy, and a genuine concern for the well-being and growth of their team members, leaders can create a culture that encourages and supports Servant Leadership.

Furthermore, it is essential to provide training and development opportunities for managers and executives to understand and embrace the Servant Leadership philosophy. This can include workshops, seminars, and mentoring programs focusing on building essential skills such as active listening, effective communication, and emotional intelligence. Organizations can empower leaders to lead with compassion and influence positive change by equipping them with the necessary tools and knowledge.

Another crucial aspect of instilling the Servant Leadership philosophy is aligning organizational systems and processes with its principles. This means integrating Servant Leadership into performance appraisal systems, reward structures, and decision-making frameworks. Organizations can encourage employees at all levels to adopt this philosophy and contribute to its success by creating an environment that recognizes and rewards behaviors aligned with Servant Leadership.

Moreover, cultivating a culture of continuous learning and improvement is vital. Encouraging employees to take risks, experiment, and learn from failures fosters a growth mindset and a willingness to serve others. Organizations can create platforms for knowledge-sharing, collaboration, and innovation, allowing employees to develop their skills and contribute to overall success. Instilling the Servant Leadership philosophy in the organization requires CEOs, leaders, and managers to embrace its core principles and values. By leading by example, providing training and development opportunities, aligning organizational systems, and fostering a culture of continuous learning, organizations can create an environment that inspires excellence and drives sustainable success through Servant Leadership.

Chapter 10

Conclusion Embracing Servant Leadership for Lasting Excellence

Recap of Key Concepts and Principals

Servant Leadership is about inspiring Excellence in Managers and Executives. As CEOs, leaders, and managers, servant leadership holds immense value in transforming our organizations and positively impacting our teams and stakeholders. This section will recapitulate the key concepts and principles of servant leadership, allowing us to deepen our understanding and further enhance our effectiveness.

At its core, servant leadership is a philosophy that emphasizes the leader's responsibility to serve others, putting their needs and well-being above their own. It is a profound shift from the traditional autocratic leadership style, focusing on power and control. Instead, servant leaders work to empower their teams, foster collaboration, and facilitate the growth and development of their employees.

One of the fundamental principles of servant leadership is the importance of empathy. By genuinely understanding and empathizing with our team members, we create an environment of trust and respect. This enables us to address their needs, concerns, and aspirations effectively. Through active listening and open communication, we foster a culture of inclusivity where everyone feels valued and heard.

Another critical concept in servant leadership is the notion of stewardship. As leaders, we are not just responsible for achieving short-term goals; we are entrusted with our organizations' long-term success and well-being. By taking a servant mindset, we become stewards of our organization's resources, ensuring their efficient and ethical use. This includes nurturing a culture of sustainability in terms of financial resources and the development of our employees.

Servant leaders also recognize the importance of collaboration and empowerment. We tap into their diverse perspectives and expertise by involving our team members in decision-making and encouraging their contributions. This inclusive approach enhances creativity and innovation and fosters a sense of ownership and commitment among team members.

Lastly, servant leadership emphasizes the significance of leading by example. As CEOs, leaders, and managers, we must embody the values and principles we wish to instill in our organizations. By demonstrating integrity, humility, and a commitment to service, we inspire excellence and motivate our teams to follow suit.

The Servant's Leader Playbook:

A Guide to Effective Leadership for All

Servant leadership is a powerful approach that enables CEOs, leaders, and managers to create a positive and impactful work environment. By practicing empathy, stewardship, collaboration, and leading by example, we inspire excellence in ourselves and others. Embracing servant leadership principles leads to enhanced employee engagement, improved organizational performance, and a more fulfilling and successful leadership journey.

A Parting Word

The role of a leader has evolved significantly. Gone are the days when leaders were solely responsible for giving orders and expecting their subordinates to follow without question. Being a servant leader is a change in your business lifestyle.

Practice the principles you have read in this book, such as

93

active listening. Leaders who genuinely listen to their employees' concerns, ideas, and aspirations build trust and make their team members feel valued. This fosters a sense of belonging and empowers individuals to contribute their best work, increasing productivity and job satisfaction.

Promote personal growth and development. By providing opportunities for skill-building, mentoring, and coaching, leaders can empower their employees to reach their full potential. This not only benefits the individuals but also contributes to the overall growth and success of the organization.

Lead by example, demonstrate integrity, ethical decision-making, and a solid commitment to their team and the organization's mission. By embodying these values, leaders inspire employees to align their actions with the organization's core principles, fostering a culture of integrity and trust.

Cultivate a culture of servant leadership, and prioritize well-being and satisfaction. Foster a positive work environment, promoting work-life balance and recognizing and appreciating individual and team achievements. By adopting this approach, leaders can create an environment that empowers employees, fosters collaboration, and drives organizational excellence.

Embracing servant leadership benefits the employees and contributes to the organization's long-term success and sustainability. As a result, managers and executives become more effective in leading their teams and can create a positive work culture that drives organizational success.

Furthermore, servant leadership enhances managers' and executives' personal growth and professional development. By focusing on the growth and well-being of their employees, leaders are naturally inclined to invest in their growth as well. They become more self-aware, empathetic, and emotionally intelligent, which is essential for effective leadership.

In addition to personal growth, servant leadership has a transformative effect on the organizational culture. By embodying servant leadership principles, managers and executives inspire their employees to adopt the same mindset. This creates a ripple effect throughout the organization, leading to a culture of collaboration, trust, and accountability. Such a culture fosters innovation, creativity, and high employee engagement, ultimately driving organizational excellence. Servant leadership has a profound and long-lasting impact on managers and executives. It enables them to develop strong and authentic leadership skills, fosters personal growth and professional development, and transforms organizational culture. Therefore, embracing servant leadership is not only beneficial for employees but also for the success and sustainability of the organization as a whole.

Remember, as a CEO, leader, or manager, you drive success and foster excellence within your organization. This book is a general guide. The approaches within can be tailored to your specific content and structure preferences, providing you with the perfect playbook as you embark on your journey toward becoming an exceptional servant leader.

Made in the USA
Columbia, SC
01 September 2023

22296572R00057